Infallible
Pope

Key to Unity or Source of Division?

Eddie L. Hyatt

Hyatt Press * 2024
Grapevine, Texas 76051

*Publish, and set up a standard;
Publish and conceal not (Jeremiah 50:2)*

Infallible Pope
By Eddie L. Hyatt

© 2024 by Hyatt International Ministries, Inc. ALL RIGHTS RESERVED.

Published by Hyatt Press
A Subsidiary of Hyatt Int'l Ministries, Inc.

Mailing Address (2024)
    Hyatt Int'l Ministries
    P. O. Box 3877
    Grapevine, TX 76099-3877

Internet Addresses
    Email: dreddiehyatt@gmail.com
    Website: www.eddiehyatt.com

Unless otherwise indicated, all Scripture quotations are taken from the New Kings James Version of the Bible. © 1979, 1980, 1982 by Thomas Nelson, Inc. Publishers.

ISBN: 978-1-888435-71-9

Printed in the United States of America

Table of Contents

Preface

Chapter 1   Is the Pope Infallible?   6

Chapter 2   No Basis in Scripture   10

Chapter 3   The Church Moves from Service to Power   17

Chapter 4   The Fabled Donation of Constantine   27

Chapter 5.   The African Church Resists Papal Power   31

Chapter 6   The Eastern Church Resists Papal Power   35

Chapter 7   The Historical Origins of Papal Infallibility   40

Chapter 8   The Reformation   45

Chapter 9   The Church Must Return to Jesus   55

Selected Bibliography   60

About the Author   62

Other Books by Author   63

Preface

In east Texas where I live, Roman Catholic Bishop, Joseph Strickland, was recently removed from his parish and office by Pope Francis. No reason was given for his removal, but those familiar with the situation knew it was because of his sharp and vocal criticisms of Pope Francis.

Strickland has been a prolife, profamily activist, leading protests against abortion, drag queens, and the radical LGBTQ agenda. When he perceived that Francis had gone soft on these issues, he roundly criticized him, even accusing him of "undermining the deposit of faith."

He was given the opportunity to resign but replied in a letter that he could not resign for that would be abandoning the congregation he had been charged to lead. Pope Francis then removed him and replaced him with someone more loyal and submissive.

As an outside Protestant observer, what struck me as strange and unreasonable about this situation was that a Argentinian pope residing in Rome could have such power over a congregation in the relatively small town of Tyler in east Texas.

In the following pages I purport to show that such centralized authority would also be strange to Peter, John, and Paul. It would also be strange to the church for at least the first four centuries of its existence.

My purpose in writing this book is not to bash Catholics or even the pope. Protestant leaders are also guilty of pursuing power and thereby doing damage to the body of Christ. I am addressing here the issue of papal infallibility because it represents the most blatant grab for power in church history. My purpose is to show how a ruinous preoccupation with power in Christian history has divided the church and quenched the work of the Holy Spirit.

In the Charismatic Renewal of the 1970s, Catholics and Protestants experienced sweet fellowship with one another under the banner of "Jesus is Lord" and in the power of the Holy Spirit. Church loyalties were transcended by a love for Jesus and openness to the work of the Holy Spirit in their midst.

I believe that such can happen again, but not so long as we are tied to a doctrine that binds us to human control. Jesus said, *The Spirit blows where He wishes* (John 3:8). History shows that the wind of the Spirit blows both inside and outside our church institutions. We cannot confine the Spirit to our liturgies, doctrines and programs.

I am indebted to many authors and theologians for the contents of this book, but I must especially single out the late, Dr. Hans Kung, the most widely read Catholic theologian in the world today. His historical treatises have been incredibly enlightening, and essential in formulating the message of this book.

I pray that God will use this book to bring new freedom and openness to the work of His Spirit throughout the church today, both Catholic and Protestant.

Chapter I
Is the Pope Infallible?

> *The road [to infallibility] was built with an unflagging Roman concern for power, which did not hesitate even over the use of forgeries.*
> Hans Kung, Catholic theologian

Is the Pope Infallible? Is he divinely protected from error in his official duties? Is he truly the Vicar of Christ with authority over all of Christendom? Is recognizing his authority the key to Christian unity?

No issue has been more historically divisive than the claims of the Roman bishop (the pope) of having authority over all Christendom. These historical claims of papal preeminence are based on the idea of Peter's primacy among the apostles, and the popes being Peter's successors and inheriting Peter's preeminence and authority.

These papal claims of power culminated with the dogma of papal infallibility being declared in 1870 by the Vatican I Council. According to this council, the pope is preserved from the possibility of error,

> When, in the exercise of his office as shepherd and teacher of all Christians, in virtue of his supreme apostolic authority, he defines a doctrine concerning faith or morals to be held by the whole Church.

In challenging the dogma of papal infallibility, it is important that we separate the person from the office. There have been good popes in the history of the Catholic Church and there have been some very wicked, even warring, popes. There have been popes who were declared heretics by later popes and popes like John Paul II who cooperated with Ronald Reagan and Margaret Thatcher to bring down the old Soviet, communist empire.

In this volume we are not dealing with individual popes, but with the papal office, which has a long and problematic history often associated with scandal, deceit, and love for power. This is why the late, Dr. Hans Kung, who served for many years as a professor at the University of Tubingen and was a theological adviser at Vatican II, states that the long road leading to Vatican I,

> Was built with an unflagging Roman concern for power, which did not hesitate even over the use of forgeries.[1]

The Catholic priest and theologian, the late Henri Nouwen, agreed with Kung and in discussing why so many people have left the Catholic Church in recent years, he blamed it on the pursuit of power by church leaders. He wrote,

> When I ask myself the main reason for so many people having left the Church during the past decades in France, Germany, Holland, and also in Canada and America, the word "power" easily

---

[1] Han Kung, *Christianity: Essence, History, and Future* (New York: Continuum, 1994), 319).

comes to mind. One of the greatest ironies of the history of Christianity is that its leaders constantly gave in to power even though they continued to speak in the name of Jesus, who did not cling to His divine power but emptied Himself and became as we are.[2]

It is worth noting that Vatican I was not an ecumenical council in the strict sense of the word. The word "ecumenical" is from the Latin *oecumenicus* meaning "worldwide." The Eastern Orthodox recognize only seven ecumenical councils all occurring before the split between the churches of the East and West in 1054. Protestants tend to be indifferent to church councils but would recognize only those same seven councils as representing the worldwide church.

Neither the Eastern Orthodox nor the Protestant churches of the Reformation participated in Vatican I. Is it not, therefore, arrogant and unreasonable for Rome to assume it has the right to force a doctrine on churches that had no say or participation in the formulation of that doctrine?

Not only Protestants and Eastern Orthodox, but many Catholics today are questioning the Catholic doctrine of papal infallibility. I have no animosity toward Catholics and have experienced sweet fellowship with Catholic brothers and sisters in Christ.

However, I cannot accept the Catholic dogma of the preeminent authority of the pope over Christendom and

---

[2] Henri Nouwen, *In the Name of Jesus* (New York: Crossroad, 1989), 15.

his infallibility. Such dogma clearly has no basis in either Scripture or history. As will be seen in the following chapters, it has also been the greatest barrier to ecumenism (Christian unity) within Christendom.

Chapter 2

No Basis in Scripture

> *Neither Christ nor his apostles prescribed any form of church government.*
> John Wesley
> Founder of Methodism

Jesus warned the Twelve, including Peter, against adopting honorific titles that would set them apart from one another. Referring to titles used by the Jewish leaders of that day, He admonished,

> But you, do not be called "Rabbi": for One is your teacher, the Christ, and you are all brethren. Do not call anyone on earth your "father;" for One is your Father, He who is in heaven. And do not be called "teachers;" for One is your Teacher, the Christ. But he who is greatest among you shall be your servant (Matthew 23:8-11).

This is why, in the New Testament, we find no sign of hierarchy in the leadership of the church. Words that carried connotations of authority such as *archon* (ruler), *timē* (rank), and *despot* (master) are used of Jewish and secular rulers but are glaringly missing in regard to Christian leaders.

A Servant Model of Leadership

Instead, *diakonos*, a word meaning "servant," with no connotations of power, status, or rank, is used of leaders in the church. *Diakonos* is the word Jesus used when He rebuked the Twelve, including Peter, when they were arguing over who would be the greatest. He said to them, *Whoever desires to become great among you, let him be your servant (diakonos)* (Mark 10:35-45).

Diakonos is also the word so often used by Paul for himself and his co-workers. To the Corinthian believers who were putting apostles and preachers on pedestals and building cliques around them, Paul declared, *Who is Paul, and who is Apollos, but diakonoi (servants) through who you believed*. Commenting on this fact, Kung has said,

> In the New Testament, not only is the word "hierarchy" consistently and deliberately avoided, but so too are all secular words for "office" in connection with church functions, as they express a relationship of power. Instead of this, an all-encompassing term, *diakonia*, service (really 'serving at table'), is used, which can nowhere evoke associations with any authority, control or position of dignity and power. [3]

Contrary to the *diakonos* model laid out by Jesus, those advocating papal infallibility emphasize the primacy of Peter among the apostles and his preeminence and authority over the Church. They also insist that this authority of Peter has been passed along to the popes through a mechanical, religious rite called apostolic succession.

These beliefs have led to the bishop of Rome adopting honorific titles such as "Vicar of Jesus Christ," "Successor of the Prince of the Apostles" and "Supreme

---

[3] Kung, *Christianity: Essence, History and Future*, 321-22.

Pontiff of the Universal Church," which are so out of character with Jesus and the New Testament.

The Church is Built on Jesus Christ

Matthew 16:18-19 is used by papal advocates to claim that Jesus said He would build His church on Peter and that He gave Peter the keys of authority over the Church. It is clear, however, from even a cursory examination of this passage, that the church is not built on Peter, but on Peter's revelation of who Jesus is, *i.e.*, on Jesus Himself.

This is clearly borne out in Jesus' response to Peter's revelation of Him as the Christ, the Son of the Living God. Jesus commends Peter for his revelation, saying,

> *Blessed are you Simon, son of Jonah, for flesh and blood did not reveal this to you, but my Father who is in heaven. And I say to you that you are Peter (petros), and on this rock (petra) I will build My church, and the gates of Hades shall not prevail against it.*

The Greek word for "Peter" in this passage is *petros*, which referred to a little rock or pebble. The Greek word for "rock" in this passage is *petra* and it was used to refer to a large massive stone. With a play on these words, Matthew records Jesus as saying, "You are *petros* (a little rock), and on this *petra* (a massive rock) I will build my Church.

The foundation on which Jesus said he would build His Church is not a little rock like Peter, but the massive rock—the *petra*--which is the revelation of who He is, *i.e.*, Himself. Also, the word "you" in vs. 19 concerning the keys of the kingdom is plural, indicating that the keys are given to the church, not solely to Peter.

That the church is built on Christ Himself is affirmed by Paul in I Corinthians 3:11. Commenting on his founding of the church in Corinth, Paul makes it clear that he did not found that church on either Peter or himself. He wrote, *For no other foundation can anyone lay than that which is laid, which is Jesus Christ.*

This was the belief of the church throughout the early centuries. For example, Saint Augustine (354-430), often acclaimed as the greatest of the church fathers, understood the rock to be, not Peter, but Christ. Commenting on this passage, he wrote,

> "Therefore," He saith, "Thour art Peter; and upon this Rock" which thou hast confessed, upon this Rock which thou hast acknowledged, saying, "Thou art the Christ, the Son of the Living God, I will build My Church;" that is upon Myself, "the Son of the living God, will I build My Church."[4]

Interestingly, this was also confirmed by Pope Benedict XVI, who as the young Joseph Ratzinger, wrote in his doctoral dissertation, "If the church is founded on Peter, it is not founded on his person, but on his faith . . . the foundation of the church is Christ."

No Primacy of Peter in the New Testament

That Peter held no special primacy among the apostles is clearly borne out in the words of Jesus to him after His resurrection as recorded in John 21:15-25. While Jesus is

---

[4] Augustine, "Sermons on New Testament Lessons," vol. 6 of *Nicene and Post-Nicene Fathers* (Peabody, MA: Hendrickson, 2004), 340.

instructing Peter to *feed My sheep*, Peter turns toward John and says to Jesus, *What about this man?*

With a stern rebuke, Jesus replied, *If I will that he remain until I come, what is that to you? You follow Me.* In other words, there were things about other believers that did not concern Peter. John had a relationship with Jesus that was of no concern to Peter. Peter must give himself to his own task and not meddle in the affairs of others. When he would involve himself with matters that were of no concern to him, he could expect to hear the voice of the Master saying, *What is that to you? You follow Me.*

Other passages of Scripture make it clear that Peter held no special primacy among the apostles. Consider, for example, that when Peter went to Antioch and waffled concerning the equal acceptance of the Gentiles in Christ, Paul publicly rebuked him in front of the church because, as Paul said, *he was to be blamed* (Galatians 2:11). Peter obviously accepted this rebuke for he knew he was in the wrong.

It is also clear that although Peter is the chief spokesman in the early chapters of Acts, it is obvious that James became the leader of the church in Jerusalem. In the first Church Council of Acts 15, in which Peter participated, it is obvious that James is presiding. After everyone has had their say about whether Gentile believers in Jesus must be circumcised and keep the Law of Moses, it is James who gives the summary statement and the position the Council will take in the matter.

It is also worth noting that the letter formulated to express the determination of this council is from neither Peter nor Paul No individual name is mentioned. The letter begins, *The apostles, the elders, and the brethren to the brethren who of the Gentiles in Antioch, Syria, and Cilicia . . ..*

It is also worth noting that there is no evidence that Peter founded the church in Rome. The idea that Peter founded this church is based on dogma, not historical evidence. In Paul's letter to the church at Rome, written probably in the fall of A.D. 57, he makes no mention of Peter, a bishop, nor any leader. Instead, he addresses the letter, *To all who are in Rome, beloved of God, called to be saints.*

At the end of the letter, Paul sends greetings to numerous people, including *Priscilla and Aquilla and the church that is in their house* (Romans 16:3-5). He also greets Andronicus and Junia whom he says, *are of note among the apostles* (Romans 16:7). He also greets others who are obviously leaders in the Roman church.

Nowhere in the letter does Paul mention Peter. This strongly indicates that Peter had no part in the founding of the church at Rome, for Paul would certainly have mentioned him if such were the case. The church was most likely founded by some of the many pilgrims from Rome who were in Jerusalem for the Feast of Pentecost when the Holy Spirit was poured out in such a dramatic fashion (Acts 2:1-12).

It is also important to note that Peter is never mentioned in Scripture with any special title or commendation. In I Corinthians 1:12, Paul rebuked the Corinthains for building cliques around himself, Apollos, and Peter. He admonished them, saying, *Now I say this that each of you says, "I am of Paul" or "I am of Apollos" or "I am of Cephas [Peter]" or "I am of Christ."*

These were cliquish groups who had turned these apostles into celebrities and played them off, one against the other. The ones who said "I am of Christ" did so, not from a sense of reverence and worship, but from a clannish competition with the other groups.

This is made plain by Paul challenging them with certain questions: *Is Christ divided? Was Paul crucified for you? Or were you baptized in the name of Paul?* In other words, by giving honor to Paul, Apollos, and Peter that belonged only to Christ, the Corinthians were creating division. And is that not happening in the church today?

No Church Order Laid Down by the Apostles

The idea of the primacy of Peter is glaringly missing from the New Testament. It can only be explained as a development of later history that papal advocates seek to impose back on Scripture. It has no basis in either Scripture or early Christianity. Oxford professor, Burnett H. Streeter was correct when he wrote,

> Whatever else is disputable, there is, I submit, one result from which there is no escape. In the primitive church there was no single system of church order laid down by the apostles. During the first hundred years of Christianity, the Church was an organism alive and growing— changing its organization to meet changing needs. Uniformity was a later development.[5]

---

[5] Burnett H. Streeter, *The Primitive Church* (New York: MacMillan, 1929), 267-68.

Chapter 3

The Church Moves from Service to Power

> *Nothing is to be gained by concealing the fact . . . that a frightening gulf separates the Church of today from the original constitution of the Church.*
> Hans Kung

The Church of the New Testament was a movement that relied on the dynamic empowering presence of the Holy Spirit for its life, community and mission, rather than organizational structure. Leadership was functional in nature and leaders saw themselves as called by the risen Christ to "serve" His people.

Organizational structure in the New Testament tended to be practical, temporal and task oriented. In the 1st century, organizational order and structure were *means* for advancing the gospel and facilitating the work of the Spirit, not *ends* in themselves to be sought and guarded. Church organization changed from place to place and in the same place at different times. Dr. David Scholer, late Professor of New Testament at Fuller Theological Seminary, wrote,

> The New Testament does not often, if at all, discuss church governance and office directly for their own sake. The texts that mention "office"

and ordination in the New Testament are particular to the situation, partial or even ambiguous, not easily correlated with any later church practice or tradition.[6]

A Spirit-Led Movement

Words used to describe leaders in the New Testament, such as apostle, pastor, bishop, etc., were functional in nature describing the leaders' task, rather than official describing their status. They were never used as titles. In Acts, for example, Luke mentions Paul by name more than 120 times and not once does he say "Apostle Paul," but merely "Paul." In 2 Peter 3:14, Peter refers to *our beloved brother Paul*. In Rev. 1:9, John the apostle, in his letter to the churches, refers to himself as *your brother and companion in tribulation*.

This obvious avoidance of titles is understandable in light of the words of Jesus in Matt. 23:6-12 where He warned His disciples about adopting titles that would set themselves apart from other believers. Both Acts and Paul's letters, the Corinthian letters in particular, indicate that the assembled churches relied on the spontaneity of the Spirit rather than on official authority for the life and direction of their meetings.

These facts led Hans von Campenhausen to describe the early church's vision of Christian community as "one of free fellowship, developing through the living interplay of spiritual gifts and ministries, without the benefit of

---

[6] David Scholer, "Patterns of Authority in the Early Church," vol. 1 of *Authority and Governance in the Evangelical Covenant Church* (Chicago: Covenant Publ., 1993), 27.

official authority or responsible elders."[7] Kung concurs suggesting that the church at Corinth "knew of neither *episkopoi* (bishops) nor *presbuteros* (elders) nor any kind of ordination but only the free and spontaneous charisms."[8] He then points out that, according to Paul in I Cor. 1:7, they were provided with all that was necessary.

It is obvious that the New Testament writers show little or no interest in order and structure for their own sake. When they do comment on structure it is to describe rather than prescribe, and what they describe varies from church to church. Commenting on this diversity, New Testament specialist, the late Dr. Gordon Fee, says, "This is hardly the stuff from which one can argue with confidence as to how the early church was organized—or whether it was!"[9]

The Institutionalization of Early Christianity

But as the first generation of Christians passed from the scene, more and more emphasis was placed on organizational structure and formality. This preoccupation with organization is known as "institutionalism" and is defined as "an emphasis on organization at the expense of other factors." In the Church, such an emphasis, or

---

[7] Hans von Campenhausen, *Ecclesiastical Authority and Spiritual Power in the Churches of the First Three Centuries* (Stanford, CA: Stanford University, 1969), 58.

[8] Hans Kung, "What Is the Essence of Apostolic Succession?," *Apostolic Succession: Rethinking A Barrier To Unity*, ed. Hans Kung (New York: Paulist Press, 1968), 35.

[9] Gordon D. Fee, *Gospel and Spirit: Issues in New Testament Hermeneutics* (Peabody, MA: Hendrickson, 1991), 121.

over-emphasis, on organization always comes at the expense of the life and freedom of the Holy Spirit.

As the Church sought more permanent forms of "church" and "worship," this led to functions of leadership being turned into offices and worship being formalized and ritualized. This eventually led to the ministry of the apostle being absorbed into the office of the bishop and bishops claiming to have inherited the authority of the apostles to teach and interpret the Scriptures.

In the New Testament, however, a bishop was simply an elder who had certain responsibilities of oversight in the Christian community, and this is borne out by the etymology of the word.

The New Testament Bishop

The word *bishop* is derived from the Greek word *episcopas*, which in its verb form means "to watch over" and, therefore, "to superintend" or "to oversee." Not unique to the New Testament, it was used in the larger Greco-Roman world of the first century in reference to individuals who functioned as tutors, inspectors, scouts, watchmen and superintendents. In the New Testament Church, the word was used to describe the function of oversight given to certain individuals in matters related to the churches. Acts 20:17, 28 and Titus 1:5–7 show that the word was used interchangeably with *prebuteros* (elder) and *poimen* (pastor), confirming the functional nature of the word.

In the New Testament church, *episcopas* was obviously about "responsibility" rather than "power." Even as late as the 5th century, the famous African church father, Augustine, alluded to I Timothy 3:1 and pointed out that the *episcopate* is a "work," not an "honor." He went on to explain that the original meaning of *episcopas* is related to responsibility, not authority. "Therefore," said Augustine, "He who loves to govern rather than do good is no bishop."[10]

Nonetheless, with the growing emphasis on organizational structure, *episcopas* (bishop) evolved into a separate and distinct office with increasing prestige and power. This change is borne out in the writings of Ignatius, bishop of Caesarea, who in all his writings (ca. A.D. 110) seems preoccupied with defending and promoting the authority and prestige of the bishop.

Dr. James L. Ash Jr. describes Ignatius's attempt to garner such authority for himself and for the office of the bishop as "a novelty."[11] Indeed, when compared with the writings of the New Testament, it is obvious that Ignatius has taken a new path in church government. Streeter says,

> What nobody questions, nobody defends; overenthusiastic defense implies the existence of strong opposition. The principle which Ignatius is so concerned to uphold is one by no means

---

[10] Augustine, "The City of God," vol. 2 of *Nicene and Post-Nicene Fathers* (Peabody, MA: Hendrickson, 2004), 413.
[11] James L. Ash Jr., "The Decline of Ecstatic Prophecy in the Early Church," *Theological Studies* 37 (1976), 249.

universally recognized.[12]

This was an obvious power grab on the part of Ignatius and history demonstrates that the power trend he advocated continued. With bishops now emerging in various cities, the bishop of Rome was, at first, looked upon as a first among equals. This became especially true after the destruction of the city of Jerusalem in A.D. 70.

The Roman bishops, however, pressed their demand for preeminence claiming to be head over the church founded by Peter and Paul. Claiming also to have inherited the apostolic authority of Peter, the chief apostle, their demands for power paved the way for the papal office and for the pope to be the spiritual counterpart of the political head-of-state, the Roman emperor.

Constantine and the Accelerated Institutionalization of the Church

The conversion of Constantine in A.D. 312 accelerated the institutionalization of the church and its transformation from a Spirit-led movement into a hierarchical religious system. In A.D. 313, Constantine issued the "Edict of Milan," a decree not only permitting freedom of worship to all inhabitants of the empire, but also granting special favors to the church. He began funneling money into the church treasuries and paying the salaries of the bishops whom he exalted into

---

[12] Streeter, *The Primitive Church*, 169–70.

positions parallel to the provincial governors of the Roman Empire.

Constantine also involved himself directly in the affairs of the Church, thereby setting the stage for the amalgamation of the powers of the church and state. In A.D. 325, for example, he called what some consider to be the "first" General Council of the Christian Church. Bishops from all parts of the empire convened in Nicea, a city in Asia Minor, at government expense. Constantine himself presided over the first session, and in later sessions he intervened at significant points in the discussions even though he had not yet been baptized. Kung says,

> Constantine used this first council not least to adapt the church organization to the state organization. The church provinces were to correspond to the imperial provinces, each with a metropolitan and a provincial synod. In other words, the empire now had its imperial church![13]

How far the church had removed itself from Jesus! And the institutionalization continued, resulting in the church becoming more and more a complex religious system with a multitude of offices, titles and regulations, all foreign to the New Testament. This is what Martin Luther was referring to when centuries later he wrote,

> That we now have bishops, rectors, priests,

---

[13] Hans Kung, *Christianity: Essence, History, and Future* (New York: Continuum, 1996), 180.

chaplains, canons, monks, and other similar titles signifying a difference in office should not surprise us; it has all come from our habit of so interpreting Scripture that not a word of it retains its true meaning. Therefore God and His Scriptures know nothing of bishops as we now have them. These things are all a result of man-made laws and ordinances.[14]

Christianity Becomes Romanized

The elevation of Christianity to official status as the religion of the Empire brought a political cohesion to the church it had previously not known. A universal system of church government began to emerge, and it soon became clear that it reflected the prevailing political pattern of the Roman Empire and was rooted in "power." And this emphasis on "power" led to many fierce political church struggles and some were quite fierce.

For example, at the Council of Ephesus in A.D. 449, physical violence broke out among the attending bishops and the presiding bishop, Flavian, died from the wounds received at this council. Gregory of Nazianzus (325-389), Patriarch of Constantinople, came to disdain Church Councils, writing,

> For my part, if I am to write the truth, my inclination is to avoid all assemblies of bishops, because I have never seen any council come to a good end, nor turn out to be a solution of evils.

---

[14] Martin Luther, "Martin Luther's Answer to Emser of Leipzig," vol. 3 of *Works of Martin Luther*, 6 vols. (Grand Rapids: Baker, 1982), 323.

On the contrary, it usually increases them. You always find there love of contention and love of power which beggar description.[15]

Basil of Caesarea, Bishop of Cappadocia (A.D. 370–379), likened the strife in the church to a great naval battle being fought by men who "cherish a deadly hate against one another."[16] He wrote,

> But what storm at sea was ever so wild and fierce as this tempest of the churches. In it every landmark of the Fathers has been moved; every foundation, every bulwark of opinion has been shaken; everything buoyed up on the unsound is dashed about and shaken down. We attack one another. If our enemy is not the first to strike us, we are wounded by the comrade at our side.[17]

In such a state, it is not surprising that the miraculous gifts of the Holy Spirit, which Paul taught were to function within the context of Christian love, became extinct in the institutional church. The church's pursuit of earthly affluence and power marked the end of the Holy Spirit's dynamic presence as the basis of its corporate life and ministry. A. J. Gordon, Baptist pastor and founder of Gordon College in Boston, was correct when he wrote,

> It is not altogether strange that when the Church forgot her citizenship in heaven and began to

---

[15] J Stevenson, ed., *Creeds, Councils, and Controversies* (London: S.P.C.K. Holy Trinity Church, 1972), 150.
[16] Basil, "On the Spirit," vol. 7 of *Nicene and Post-Nicene Fathers of the Christian Church*, 48.
[17] Ibid., 49.

establish herself in luxury and splendor on earth, she should cease to exhibit the supernatural gifts of heaven.[18]

The institutionalization of the church and the centralizing of "power" in the office of "bishop" continued with little deep thought and consideration as to how this compared to Jesus and the New Testament. With the exception of the monastics who withdrew from society and retreated to the deserts for prayer and meditation, most Christians, especially the bishops, preferred to enjoy the power and perks that came with being the official state religion.

---

[18] A. J. Gordon, *The Ministry of Healing* (Harrisburg, PA: Christian Publ., 1961), 64.

Chapter 4
The Fabled Donation of Constantine

> *The constitution of the Church was, in the main, modeled on the organization of the Empire.*
> Rudolph Sohm

The development of the papal office has been a long and problematic process that encountered much opposition along the way and was never accepted by all of Christendom. In fact, the ancient churches of the East (now known as the Eastern Orthodox) never accepted the authoritative claims of the bishop of Rome (the pope) in the West.

Just like small, independent charismatic churches today will often align themselves with a big-city, mega church and its charismatic pastor, churches after the 2nd century were willing to offer a certain honor and respect to the church in Rome because of its size and location in the capital of the Empire.

However, when attempts were made by Roman bishops to exercise authority over other churches, they were met with outright opposition in the West, the East, and in North Africa. This opposition will be delineated in subsequent chapters; but suffice it to say that history shows that papal claims of preeminence and authority were vehemently opposed by other churches. The opposition was so great, in fact, that Rome resorted to lies and forgeries to buttress its claims of universal preeminence and authority.

The Donation of Constantine

When Dr. Kung referred to the use of "forgeries" to buttress papal power, he was referring, in particular, to the "Donation of Constantine," which was used, beginning in the 8th century, to further establish the preeminence of the Roman bishop. According to this fable, Constantine, the persecutor of Christians, was smitten with leprosy and then healed by Pope Silvester who also converted him and baptized him.

According to this legend, when Constantine later decided to move the capital to Constantinople without papal approval, he soon realized his sin and came and prostrated himself before Pope Silvester. When his sin was forgiven, he then moved the capital to Constantinople with the pope's consent.

According to this myth, before departing, Constantine then bestowed on Silvester the right to wear the Roman imperial insignia and robes and bequeathed to him Rome and all the provinces and cities in Italy and the western regions. In other word, Constantine bestowed on the Roman bishop a kingly royalty and authority like that of an emperor over all the cities and churches of the West.

Popes latched on to this fable and it became the basis for the papal throne and the pope's royal insignia, garments, entourage and crown. It became the basis for popes exercising civil as well as spiritual authority.

In addition, the story implied that Constantine had received his authority for establishing the Byzantine empire of the East from the bishop of Rome. This was used by later popes to claim universal authority over all churches everywhere, even those of Byzantine.

Found to be False

It was not until the 15th century that this story was challenged by the Catholic official and historian, Lorenzo Valla. The Donation of Constantine is now widely recognized, even by Catholic historians, as fictitious. Nonetheless, it served its purpose in providing a powerful argument for the medieval popes to further their claims of universal preeminence and authority.

These facts, uncovered by Catholic historians, also serve to demonstrate how the pomp and pageantry of the modern papacy is rooted, not in Jesus and the New Testament, but in ancient, imperial Rome.

Indeed, after Constantine, the Church became Romanized, leading Rudolph Sohm to say, "The constitution of the Church was, in the main, modeled on the organization of the Empire."[19] And the late Cardinal Leon Joseph Suenens admitted,

> When I was young the Church was presented to us as a hierarchical society: it was described as "juridicially perfect," having within itself all the powers necessary to insure and promote its own existence. This view reflected an image of the Church which was closely modeled on civil, and

---

[19] Rudolph Sohm, *Outlines of Church History*, (London: MacMillan, 1913), 47.

even military, society.[20]

After Constantine, the bishops were generally looked upon as the successors of the apostles and the bishop of Rome as the successor of Peter, the chief of the apostles. They began dressing in imperial regalia, surrounded by Romish pomp and ceremony. This was based, not on Scripture, but on Roman imperial custom and law. Kung has commented on this, saying,

> Bishops were accorded secular titles, insignia and privileges which up to then had been reserved for the emperor or high officials: candles, incense, a throne, shoes, the maniple, the pallium and so on.[21]

What seemed to many at the time as a wonderful development within the church, is now seen as a spiritual fall with the church becoming dependent, not on the power of the Gospel, but on a grandiose form and ritual and on the power of the state to enforce its doctrines and practices.

---

[20] Leon Joseph Cardinal Suenens, *A New Pentecost?* (New York: Seabury Press, 1975), 15.

[21] Kung, *The church*, 526.

Chapter 5

The African Church Resists Papal Power

> *It may be that the line of advance for the Church of today is not to imitate the forms, but to recapture the spirit of the primitive Church.*
> Burnett H. Streeter,
> Oxford Professor

Around A.D. 250 a Church synod in Spain deposed two leaders for certain lapses and trespasses. When the two deposed individuals traveled to Rome and appealed to the Roman bishop, he reversed the decision of the Spanish synod. When a conflict arose in Spain over whether the sentence of the Roman bishop should be recognized, the Spanish Christians asked the bishops of North Africa for their opinion.

The African bishops met in a synod and concluded that the Roman bishop was wrong and encouraged the Spanish Church leaders to stand by their decision and not yield to the "unjust" edict from Rome. They also declared the decision of the Roman bishop to be void.

They insisted that the church in each city, in communion with other churches, had the right to make final decisions concerning its own affairs. They clearly rejected the idea of centralized controlling authority, such as the papacy, in the church.

31

Although the issue was never completely resolved, the actions of the Spanish and African Christians illustrates that the authority of the Roman bishop was by no means universally recognized at this early time.

Cyprian Opposes Pope Stephanas

In a later controversy between Africa and Rome, the Roman bishop, Stephanas, claimed his unique authority as Peter's successor and sought to excommunicate several of the African churches. The noted church father, Cyprian (195-258), bishop of Carthage, rejected his claim and accused Stephanas of introducing innovations into the church and thereby disrupting the church's unity. The innovations Cyprian referred to were the Roman bishop's claim of authority over churches in other regions.

Cyprian claimed equal dignity with Stephanas and addressed him as "dearest brother." He also reproved Stephanas for the pursuit of power by the Roman bishops, saying, "No one should make himself a bishop of bishops."

He also admonished Stephanas to be teachable, saying, "It is no more beneath the dignity of a Roman bishop than any other man, to suffer himself to be corrected when he is in the wrong."[22]

Augustine Rebukes Pope Zosimus

Another controversy between Rome and Africa erupted

---

[22] Augustus Neander, vol. 1 of *General History of the Christian Religion and Church*, 4 vols., trans. Joseph Torrey (Boston: Crocker & Brewster, 1853), 216.

early in the fifth century when the newly installed Roman bishop, Zosimus, took sides in a theological dispute between Augustine and the North African church with Pelagius and his followers. Pelagius emphasized human ability in salvation and apparently taught that a person could live free of sin, even apart from God's grace. His teaching contained the seeds of heresy that could undermine the need of humanity for a Savior.

Augustine wrote several works against Pelagius and was commended by the Roman bishop, Innocent. However, in A.D. 416, Innocent died and the new bishop, Zosimus, had a different perspective on the matter. Through the influence of Pelagian teachers in Rome, Zosimus issued a letter in which he commended the teachings of Pelagius and rebuked Augustine and the African bishops for not having examined the issue more closely.

In response, a synod of African bishops, including Augustine, convened in Carthage in A.D. 416. They issued an edict condemning the teachings of Pelagius. They also addressed a strongly worded letter to the Roman bishop in which they clearly delineated their position and reprimanded him for embracing false teaching.

The influence of the African bishops is shown in that the Roman bishop, after receiving the letter, carefully began to back away from his support of Pelagius. He eventually reversed his position and adopted the position of

Augustine and the African bishops.[23] Thanks to the African church and its stand for truth, Pelagianism became universally recognized for the heretical teaching that it was.

A Relentless Pursuit of Power

In spite of widespread opposition, the Roman bishops continued to push their claims of preeminence in the Church. They made much headway in establishing their claim that the bishop of Rome is the successor of Peter, the chief of the apostles, and that he has inherited Peter's dignity and authority. This was seen as an "office," so that even though the bishop of Rome may not possess Peter's character and virtue, he does, it was argued, in a legal sense inherit his authority.

Siricius, who served as the Roman bishop from 384-99, was the first to call himself "Pope." "Pope" comes from *papas* a word meaning "papa" or "father" and was already in use by various leaders, despite the words of Jesus to the contrary in Matthew 23:9. Nonetheless, in his pursuit of power, Siricius claimed it as an exclusive title for himself alone. He also began referring to his edicts and declarations as "apostolic."[24]

Bishops of Rome after Siricius continued to speak of themselves alone as "pope" and it became an exclusive title expressing their sense of a unique and elite universal status.

---

[23] Augustus Neander, vol. 2 of *General History of the Christian Religion and Church*, 590-592.
[24] Kung, *Christianity: Essence, History, and Future*, 312.

Chapter 6

The Eastern Church Resists Papal Power

> *All historians today are agreed that East and West separated on the basis of a progressive alienation which coincided with the equally progressive growth of papal authority.*
>
> John Meyendorff
> Russian Orthodox Historian

In the East, the resistance to papal claims of universal authority were even more intense. Although there were cultural and doctrinal differences between the churches of the East and West, it was the authoritative claims of the bishop of Rome that led to the final rupture.

When Constantine moved the capital of the Empire from Rome to Constantinople (present day Istanbul) in A.D. 330, the vacuum of civil authority that it left was filled by the bishop of Rome who sought to buttress his claim of priority as the successor of Peter, the chief of the apostles. This, however, set the stage for ongoing power struggles between Old Rome and the New Rome of Constantinople.

In the New Rome, the emperor was supreme, even over the church; and the bishop (or "Patriarch" as he was called) was considered the spiritual leader equal to the bishop of Rome and the bishops of other large metropolitan areas such as Alexandria and Antioch.

The bishops of Rome, however, continued to press their claims of priority and authority in the church, even over the church of Constantinople. With the governmental apparatus removed to Constantinople, the Roman bishops began to levy taxes and raise armies, things that had formerly been the province of civil rulers.

Then on Christmas Eve of 800, in Saint Peter's Basilica, Pope Leo III took a decisive step that formalized and politicized the division between East and West. He autocratically crowned Charlemagne, King of the Franks, and bestowed on him the title of Emperor, a title that hitherto had been reserved for the Emperor in Constantinople. Kung says,

> The consequence was that by the pope's grace, a new Western, Germanic emperor stood alongside and confronted the sole legitimate Roman emperor in the East. In Byzantine eyes, Rome had thus finally become heretical, a view which many Eastern Christians, including theologians, maintain to the present day.[25]

The pope did not by any means consider himself to be subject to the emperor whom he had just created. He and succeeding popes pressed the argument that in the same way that the moon derives its light from the sun, so the emperor derives his authority from the pope. And this authority, it was claimed, was not limited geographically but extended over the entire earth

---

[25] Kung, *Christianity: Essence, History and Future*, 248.

including the Eastern sector of the Empire and its capital of Constantinople. Indeed, the Russian Orthodox historian, John Meyendorff, was right when he said,

> All historians today are agreed that East and West separated on the basis of a progressive alienation which coincided with the equally progressive growth of papal authority.[26]

The Division Between East and West Becomes Permanent

The divide between East and West was deepened even more when, in 1054, the papal legate, Cardinal Humbert, led a delegation to Constantinople to discuss with Patriarch Cerularius tensions over differences in the liturgies of the churches of the East and West.

Humbert, being an advocate of absolute papal power, insulted the Eastern Christians and challenged the right of the Patriarch to his title. As might be expected, the negotiations were unfruitful and Humbert, upon departing Constantinople, in an act of arrogance and self-importance, left a decree of excommunication of the Patriarch and his followers on the altar of the Church of Saint Sophia.

In response, Cerularius called a synod and excommunicated the Pope and his followers. The divide now seemed final but future events would serve to deepen even more the animosity between East and West that continues to the present day.

---

[26] Kung, *Christianity: Essence, History and Future*, 243-44.

In 1204 the armies of the Fourth Crusade, on their way to deliver the Holy Land from the Muslim Turks, passed through Constantinople. Believing the Eastern Christians to be heretics because of their separation from the pope and Rome, the crusaders attacked the city and plundered it with fire and much violence, raping the women and slaughtering its inhabitants.

With the sanction of Rome, they expelled the emperor and Patriarch from the city and replaced them with a Latin (Western) emperor and a Patriarch loyal to the pope. The churches were forced to accept the liturgies of the Roman Church, and all Greek clergy were forced to take an oath of allegiance to Rome, and all in the name of "unity."

The Fall of Constantinople to Islam

The citizens of Constantinople slowly regained control of their lives and their churches, but the rape of their city by the crusaders left them in a state of weakness and a deepened hatred of Rome. One hundred and fifty years later, with the armies of the Muslim Turks amassing on the horizon, the emperor in Constantinople, desperate for survival, signed an agreement with Rome in which he acknowledged the pope's authority in return for Rome's guarantee of military assistance against the Turks. However, 40 years later when the Turks attacked Constantinople, Rome did not send help and the city fell to the Muslim invaders who renamed it Istanbul.

Eastern Christians now found themselves under the rule of the Muslim Ottoman Turks who allowed them to exist as second-class citizens with restricted rights and subject to a special tax imposed on non-Muslims.

The hatred for Rome now ran so deep that many Eastern Christians declared that they preferred Turkish rule to that of the pope and Rome. A common saying was "Better death than Rome! Better the turban than the mitre!"[27] Even today there are many in Eastern Orthodoxy, including theologians, who believe that the fall of Constantinople to the Ottoman Turks was God's judgment on the city for entering an agreement with Rome and submitting to the authority of the pope.

---

[27] Kung, *Christianity: Essence, History and Future*, 256.

Chapter 7

The Historical Origin of Papal Infallibility

> *The doctrine was invented in the first place by a few dissident Franciscans because it suited their convenience to invent it; it was accepted by the papacy because it suited the convenience of the popes to accept it.*
>
> Brian Tierney

Although the bishops of Rome consistently expanded their claims of priority and authority from the 3rd century on, the idea of papal infallibility did not surface until the 13th century, but not by the pope. Interestingly, it was rejected by the pope and the Catholic Church at that time.

We are indebted to the Catholic historian, Brian Tierney, who has demonstrated the origins of the doctrine of papal infallibility in his book, appropriately titled, *Origins of Papal Infallibility*. Tierney demonstrates that the doctrine was first proposed in the 13th century and rejected. He notes that the doctrine is not orthodox, and may even be considered "heterodox," which is a polite way of saying "heretical."

Tierney, who is an expert in medieval church history, documents that the idea of papal infallibility was first introduced around 1280 by an eccentric Franciscan by the name of Peter Olivi. Olivi had a particular reason for formulating this doctrine. Pope Nicholas III had issued a very favorable decree in regard to the Franciscans and Olivi wanted all subsequent popes to be bound to that decree.

This novel idea of popes being infallible was not taken seriously and when, forty years later, the Franciscans tried to use it to force Pope John XXII to act favorably on their behalf, he issued a bull (official document) in which he condemned the doctrine of papal infallibility as "a work of the devil, the father of all lies."[28] The idea of papal infallibility was then dropped except for a few dissident Franciscans who tried to use it to prove that John XXII was a heretic for not affirming the favorable ruling of his predecessor.

This means that there was no widespread acceptance of papal infallibility in the Middle Ages, nor during the time leading up to Vatican I, as its proponents have claimed. Tierney says,

> There is no convincing evidence that papal infallibility formed any part of the theological or canonical tradition of the church before the thirteenth century; the doctrine was invented in the first place by a few dissident Franciscans because it suited their convenience to invent it; it was accepted by the papacy because it suited the convenience of the popes to accept it.[29]

---

[28] Brian Tierney, *Origins of Papal Infallibility*, 186-96)
[29] Tierney, *Origins of Papal Infallibility*, 281).

What About 3 Popes at One Time?

The above scenario was followed shortly thereafter by the papal schism, when there were two and then three popes at the same time. This scandalous schism began in 1305 when a Frenchman, Clement V, was elected pope but refused to move his residency to Rome. Instead, he established the papal residence and apparatus in the French city of Avignon. As a result, a total of seven popes reigned in Avignon from 1309-1377.

In 1377, Pope Gregory XI moved the papacy back to Rome, but died shortly thereafter. His successor, Urban VI, showed such mental disturbance that a group of cardinals elected another pope, Clement VII, who took up residence back in Avignon. Urban VI, however, refused to give up his papal office and so the Catholic Church had two popes, one in Rome and one in Avignon.

Each pope excommunicated the other and each condemned the other to hell. As a result, there were now two colleges of cardinals, two curias and two financial systems that, according to Kung, "duplicated the financial abuses of the papacy." In seeking to resolve the matter, the cardinals of both sides met together in Pisa in 1409 and elected a new pope, Alexander V. The former two popes, however, refused to vacate their office and the Catholic Church suddenly had three popes.

This, of course, was scandalous and led to loud calls for a reform of the Catholic Church. The problem was finally dealt with by the Council of Constance (1414-1418), which deposed all three popes and installed a new one, Martin V. In the process of dealing with this papal scandal, this council subordinated the pope's authority to its own. Concerning its own status, the council declared, "Everyone of whatever estate or dignity, even if this be papal, is bound to obey it in matters related to the faith." So great was the scandal and shame surrounding the papal office at this time that no one would have dared even suggest that the pope was infallible.

Heretical Popes in History

The opponents of papal infallibility at Vatican I marshalled impressive arguments, including the fact that at least two popes were declared heretics by later popes and councils. Pope Vigilius (500-555), for example, adopted conflicting positions about Monophysitism, which was a controversy concerning the nature of Christ.

At the beginning of his reign as pope, Vigilius supported the Monophysite position, which purported that Christ had only one divine nature, thereby denying His real humanity. This was heresy. Many believe that he took this position because it was politically advantageous for him since the empress, Theodora of Constantinople, was favorable to the Monophysites.

When, however, the political situation changed, his position on the matter changed and he opposed the Monophysites. Kung says,

> He lost all credibility because of his fickleness, so that later he was not even buried at St. Peter's,

and down through the centuries continued to be despised even in the West.[30]

Another heretical pope was Honorius I (585 638). He was condemned by the Sixth Ecumenical Council of Constantinople in 681 because he promoted the heresy of the Monothelites. The Monothelites taught that there is only one will in Christ, which was opposed by the orthodox who taught that Christ, because He is both God and human, had separate wills in his human and divine natures.

The condemnation of Honorius as a heretic was confirmed by the Seventh and Eighth Ecumenical Councils and by subsequent popes. The question presented at Vatican I was how could they declare papal infallibility when their own popes and councils had declared former popes as heretical? However, in spite of such rational barriers to the doctrine, the papal advocates were able to push through their goal of insulating the Roman bishop and the Roman Church from judgment and criticism with their dogma of papal infallibility.

---

[30] Kung, *Christianity: Essence, History, and Future*, 318).

Chapter 8

The Reformation

> *I simply taught, preached, wrote God's Word; otherwise I did nothing. The Word so weakened the papacy that never a prince or emperor did such damage to it. I did nothing. The Word did it all.*
> Martin Luther

During the Middle Ages, the papal office became fully developed with popes exercising civil as well as spiritual power. They collected taxes, raised armies, and subjugated kings and rulers. They also sold indulgences, which offered forgiveness of sins and release from purgatory, all for a price. Simony became rampant with the buying and selling of church offices. The Roman Church and the papal office thus became extremely wealthy and the most dominant force in Western society.

However, this preoccupation with earthly affluence and political power produced a spiritual dearth in the Roman Church. Illustrating this fact is a story about Thomas Aquinas (1225-74) visiting Rome and being shown that church's wealth by Pope Innocent IV.

In the course of their observations, and in an allusion to Acts 3:1-8, Innocent said to Aquinas, "You see that the Church is no longer in an age in which she can say, 'Silver and gold have I none.'" Alluding to the same passage, Aquinas replied, "It is true, nor can she say to the lame man, 'Rise up and walk.'"[31]

Forerunners of the Reformation

Many longed for a return to the Christianity of the New Testament with its freedom, simplicity, and spiritual power. This led to individuals and groups arising both inside and outside the Catholic Church advocating a return to the New Testament and rejecting the erroneous doctrines and practices that had infiltrated the church and been embraced in the name of "tradition."

Some of the better-known names who challenged the Church to return to the New Testament as its guide were Peter Waldo (1140-1218), John Wycliffe (1330-84) John Huss (1369-1415), and Martin Luther (1483-1546).

Peter Waldo, although a layman, requested permission from the Catholic Church for him and his followers to share their faith and preach the Gospel. Pope Innocent III refused their request declaring them to be, not heretics, but ignorant lay people. When Waldo refused to abide by the church's order, he was excommunicated in 1184. He and his followers then formed their own church, which they insisted was a continuation of the apostolic church of the New Testament. The Waldenses may still be found in many parts of Italy.

John Wycliffe was a Catholic priest and professor of theology at Oxford University. He has been called "the morning star of the Reformation." He believed the papacy had become corrupt and he increasingly argued

---

[31] Eddie Hyatt, *2000 Years of Charismatic Christianity* (Lake Mary, FL: Charisma House, 2002), 51.

for Scripture as the authoritative center of Christianity, that the claims of the popes were unhistorical, and that the moral unworthiness of priests invalidated their office and sacraments. He called for the pope to give up his wealth and for bishops to live simple lives as did Jesus and the early apostles. He also suggested that the pope was the Antichrist, predicted by Scripture to arise in the latter times.

He was condemned by the pope, harassed by Catholic officials, and removed from his teaching position at Oxford. However, he was never tried and convicted of heresy and continued to write in private until his death. Nonetheless, after his death, the Council of Constance declared him a heretic and ordered his bones to be dug up and burned.

John Hus (1369-1415) was a Catholic priest in what would be the present-day Czech Republic, and he served as dean and rector of Charles University in Prague. Huss got in trouble with Catholic authorities when, 100 years before Luther, he began preaching that Scripture is the ultimate authority for the Christian, not the pope. He was arrested and tried as a heretic. In 1415 the Council of Constance found him guilty of heresy, and he was burned at the stake the same day. His followers were then targeted for persecution and incarceration. Nonetheless, the movement he ignited lived on right down to the time of Martin Luther and the Reformation.

Martin Luther and the Reformation

Martin Luther (1483-1546) was a Catholic priest and professor of Bible and theology at the University of

Wittenberg in Germany. He was a devout Catholic but struggled to find peace in his heart with God. Out of this personal struggle he discovered the Biblical truth of justification by faith alone, which transformed his personal life.

This set him on a quest to discover the role of faith and Scripture in salvation and the Christian life. Over time he became convinced that the Catholic Church had been corrupted through the centuries and was in serious need of radical reform based on Scripture.

The proactive message of reform that Luther developed was threefold: (1) *sola fide* (faith alone); that we are saved by faith alone apart from church appointed indulgences, sacraments, penances and the like; (2) *sola Scriptura* (Scripture alone); that the ultimate authority for the Christian is the Bible, not the pope; and (3) *the priesthood of all believers* by which he insisted that everyone is a priest and may go to God apart from the priestly, mediatorial system of the Roman Church.

Although it is generally thought that Luther's conflict with the Roman Church was over doctrine, it really boiled down to the issue of papal authority. Luther did not want to leave the Catholic church. He wanted to see it reformed according to Scripture. However, when he was ordered by Rome to stop preaching the above doctrines, he had to decide to either obey God or the pope.

With various supporters of the pope now attacking him, Luther began the serious work of putting his thoughts in writing. In 1520 he wrote two books, *To the Christian Nobility of the German Nation* and *The Babylonian Captivity of the Church*, in which he relentlessly attacked the papal office and the Roman Church system. In *The Babylonian Captivity of the Church*, for example, he wrote,

> Therefore, no one is obliged to obey the ordinances of the pope, or required to listen to him, except when he teaches the gospel and Christ. And the pope should teach nothing but faith without any restrictions. But since Christ says, *He who hears you* (plural) *hears Me* (Luke 10:16), why does not the pope also hear others? Why does not an unbelieving pope now and then hear a believing servant of his who has the word of faith? Blindness, sheer blindness reigns among the pontiffs.[32]

Luther went even further and accused the pope of being the Antichrist. He was particularly incensed at the selling of indulgences and church offices. In his book, *To the Christian Nobility of the German Nation*, he thundered,

> If there were no other base trickery to prove that the pope is the true Antichrist, this one would be enough to prove it. Here this, O pope, not of all men the holiest but of all men most sinful! O that God from heaven would soon destroy your throne and sink it in the abyss of hell.[33]

Kung, a Catholic theologian who did his doctoral dissertation on Luther, says that Luther did not accuse

---

[32] Martin Luther, "The Babylonian Captivity of the Church," *Three Treatises* (Philadelphia: Fortress Press, 1957), 194-95.

[33] Martin Luther, "*To the Christian Nobility of the German Nation,*" *Three Treatises* (Philadelphia: Fortress Press, 1957), 194-95.

the pope of being the Antichrist out of hate. In his voluminous work, *Christianity: Essence, History and Future*, he says,

> For Luther it was now clear that such a Pope had to be the Antichrist announced in the New Testament. This insight was not just a product of Luther's polemic or hate, but was forced in on him because papal teaching and practice were contrary to the gospel.[34]

Luther Excommunicated

On June 15, 1520, Pope Leo X issued a papal bull (official decree) giving Luther sixty days to recant or be declared a heretic. Luther received the document on October 10, meaning he had had until December 10 to respond.

On the morning of December 10 Luther's students built a large bonfire. Luther then publicly burned the papal bull, the Roman canon law and other books supporting the pope. It was an open and defiant act against the pope and the Roman Church.

Leo responded by announcing Luther's formal excommunication as of January 3, 1521. He referred to Luther as "a wild boar" that had invaded the Lord's vineyard. Excommunication was also threatened against anyone who would harbor Luther or his friends.

All princes and magistrates were ordered to seize Luther and his followers and turn them over to the Roman authorities. Christians were ordered not to read, print or

---

[34] Kung, *Christianity: Essence, History, and Future*, 538.

publish any of Luther's books, but instead to burn them, and such occurred in many cities

"Here I Stand"
Luther's Bold Stand at Worms

Based on negotiations between Luther, Prince Frederick, the emperor, and religious rulers, it was agreed that Luther would appear before a civil/religious court, called a Diet, in the German city of Worms. Frederick also negotiated a "safe conduct" from the emperor meaning that he agreed not to arrest Luther in his travels to and from the Diet.

It was an impressive tribunal before which Luther was ordered to defend his teaching. The emperor in all his royal dress and entourage was there along with bishops, cardinals, personal delegates of the pope, dukes, princes and counts, all in their splendid garb and titles. Philip Schaff called it "a fair representation of the highest powers in Church and State—a numerous array of dignitaries of every rank."[35]

In contrast, Luther was dressed simply in his monk's cowl as he faced this imposing court. It was David versus Goliath multiplied a hundred times over.

A table had been placed in the room with Luther's books on it. He was first asked if these were his books. He looked them over and replied in the affirmative. He was then ordered to recant.

Luther quietly asked for more time to consider the demand of recantation. Schaff thinks his request was not

---

[35] Philip Schaff, vol. 7 of *History of the Christian Church* (Grand Rapids: Eerdmans, 1994), 300.

out of fear but out of seriousness, knowing the gravity of the situation. The emperor gave Luther one day to consider the order and he returned to his lodging where he spent much time in prayer.

During the night, there came into his heart a fearlessness and boldness such as the apostles must have experienced when they stood before the Jewish authorities and boldly defended their faith in Jesus (Acts 5:29-32). Later in life Luther wrote about that moment, saying, "I was fearless. I was afraid of nothing. God can make one so desperately bold."[36]

Luther returned the next day and was again ordered to recant. He stated that he was willing to recant but only if he could be shown by Scripture and reasonable arguments that he was wrong. Knowing his life was on the line, Luther did not flinch, but quietly and confidently stated,

> I consider myself convicted by the testimony of Holy Scripture, which is my basis. My conscience is captive to the Word of God. Thus, I cannot and will not recant anything, because acting against one's conscience is neither safe nor sound. Here I stand! I can do no other! God help me! Amen!

The proceedings were over and Luther returned to his lodgings, where he threw up his arms and joyfully shouted, "I am through, I am through!" Knowing that many "heretics" before him had been beheaded, he exclaimed, "If I had a thousand heads, I would rather

---

[36] Schaff, vol. 7 of *History of the Christian Church*, 299.

have them all cut off one by one than make one recantation."

Luther departed and, after further deliberations, the court affirmed the pope's excommunication of Luther as a heretic. Anyone knowing of his whereabouts was to inform the nearest authorities so that he could be arrested and brought to justice.

By this time, however the Reformation had gained such widespread support that neither the pope nor emperor would dare attempt an arrest of Luther and he returned to Wittenberg where he continued his teaching and writing.

In commenting on how he, a simple monk and teacher, had been able to have such an impact when opposed by both the pope and the emperor, Luther replied,

> I simply taught, preached, wrote God's Word; otherwise I did nothing. The Word so weakened the papacy that never a prince or emperor did such damage to it. I did nothing. The Word did it all.[37]

Conclusion

The major rift that took place in Christendom at the time of the Reformation was not first and foremost about doctrine, *i.e.*, justification by faith, but about the papal claim of absolute authority over all of Christendom. As in the former split between the churches of the East and the West, the division that took place at the time of the Reformation concerned the bishop of Rome's claim of

---

[37] Eddie Hyatt, *Revival Fire* (Tulsa: Hyatt Press, 2009), 86.

priority and authority in all the Church. Kung says,

> And from a historical perspective there can be no doubt that it is not Luther but Rome which bears the chief responsibility for the way in which the dispute over the right way to salvation and practical reflection on the gospel very rapidly turned into a fundamental dispute over authority in the church and the infallibility of Popes.[38]

---

[38] Kung, *Christianity: Essence, History and Future*, 538.

Chapter 9

The Church Must Return to Jesus

> *The road to unity is not the return of one Church to another, or the exodus of one Church to join another, but a common crossroads, the conversion of all Churches to Christ and thus to one another.*
>
> Han Kung

Today, even Catholic theologians are recognizing and acknowledging the damage done by the pursuits of power carried out through history by Roman bishops and their supporters. Kung, for example, considers papal claims of authority and infallibility to be the number one barrier to Christian unity. He says,

> No one can overlook the fact that with time the absolutist papacy has become the ecumenical problem number one. Paul VI was the first to concede this himself with ecumenical openness; instead of being a rock of unity, the papacy is a block on the way to ecumenical understanding.[39]

In my book, *Pursuing of Power*, I have shown how this unbiblical pursuit of power is also prevalent in Protestantism and particularly in the Pentecostal-

---

[39] Kung, *Christianity: Essence, History, and Future*, 520.

Charismatic movement of which I have been a part.[40] To see a dynamic Spiritual awakening that will impact both Catholic and Protestant, we must all learn that, in the words of Sir John Acton, "Power corrupts; absolute power corrupts absolutely."

Although I do not expect a formal change in the institutional hierarchy, I have hope that the people themselves can still make a difference. As mentioned in the Preface, in the past I have experienced sweet fellowship with Catholics around the Lordship of Jesus and in the life of the Holy Spirit. It can happen again, and will, when love for Jesus and openness to the Holy Spirit transcends church and denominational loyalties.

This happened during the Charismatic Renewal of the 1960s-70s when the Holy Spirit was poured out on the churches of all denominations. This work of the Spirit transcended denominational barriers and brought together Christians of all persuasions under the banner of "Jesus is Lord" and in the power of His Spirit.

The high-water mark of the movement was in 1977 when 52,000 met together at Arrowhead Stadium in Kansas City, Missouri. One-half of the registrants were Roman Catholic, while the other half consisted mostly of Lutherans, Presbyterians, Episcopalians, denominational Pentecostals, Baptists, Methodists and Messianic Jews. Great rejoicing filled the stands as the multitude sang and shouted praises to God.

---

[40] This book is available in paperback only from the online bookstore at www.eddiehyatt.com. It is available in kindle from Amazon.

On the platform together at one time was the General Superintendent of the Assemblies of God (white Pentecostal), the Presiding Bishop of the Church of God in Christ (black Pentecostal), a Catholic Cardinal, and Christian leaders from other churches and denominations. Cardinal Leon Joseph Suenens of Brussels, one of the participants who had experienced the baptism in the Holy Spirit, which this movement emphasized, wrote of this conference,

> It is to Christians moved by this renewal that we owe the most impressive ecumenical manifestation of our time. Catholics, Baptists, Episcopalians, Lutherans, Mennonites, Pentecostals, Presbyterians, United Methodists, Messianic Jews and a non-denominational group, greeted one another with warmth and joy and prayed together. Bearing in mind the history of strained relations between the Christian confessions in the United States, this Congress was epoch-making, the realization of an impossible dream.[41]

If we are to see Christian unity in Christendom today, Jesus Christ must be given His rightful place of centrality in all the churches. Though we may differ in doctrine, we can come together under the recognition that "He is Lord." He must be the basis of our unity, rather than a particular doctrine, church, or denomination. Kung rightly said,

> The road to unity is not the return of one Church to another, or the exodus of one Church to join

---

[41] Cardinal Leon Joseph Cardinal Suenens, *Ecumenism and Charismatic Renewal: Theological and Pastoral Orientations*, 23

another, but a common crossroads, the conversion of all Churches to Christ and thus to one another.[42]

Yes, Jesus must become front and center as he was in the church of the New Testament.[43] When we read the New Testament, we cannot help but notice that it is all about Jesus. He is the Beginning and the End. He is the First and the Last (Revelation 1:11). He is the Light of the World (John 9:5), He is the living Bread that came down from heaven (John 6:51). He is the Way, the Truth and the Life (John 14:6). In Acts 4:8-12, the apostles proclaimed to the Jewish authorities, not themselves or Peter, but Jesus, saying,

> Nor is there salvation in any other, for there is no other name under heaven given among men by which we must be saved.

Making the pope the point of unity serves only to undermine this preeminence that belongs to Jesus alone, and it is starkly at odds with the Christ-centered message of the New Testament. This centrality of Christ was summed up by C.S. Lewis who wrote,

> The Church exists for nothing else but to draw men to Christ, to make them little christs. If they are not doing that, all the cathedrals, clergy, missions, sermons, even the Bible itself, are

---

[42] Hans Kung, *The Church* (Garden City, NY: Image Books, 1976), 379.
[43] Eddie Hyatt, *Discovering the Real Jesus* (Grapevine, TX: Hyatt Press, 2023), 149.

simply a waste of time.[44]

Christian leaders, both Catholic and Protestant, must come down off their thrones and humble themselves before God and the people they purport to lead. In I Peter 5:5b-6, Peter admonishes,

> *Yes, all of you be submissive to one another, and be clothed with humility, for "God resists the proud, but gives grace to the humble." Therefore humble yourselves under the mighty hand of God, that he may exalt you in due time.*

We must all realize that we have a perfect, infallible Savior, but we are all, including the pope, frail and fallible human beings in need of God's mercy and grace. With that understanding we can come together under the banner that declares, "Jesus is Lord," and pray, "Come Holy Spirit and renew Your Church once again!"

---

[44] C. S. Lewis, *Mere Christianity* (Glasgow, England: Fount Paperbacks, 1977), 167.

Selected Bibliography

Ash, James L. Jr. "The Decline of Ecstatic Prophecy in the Early Church," *Theological Studies* 37, 1976.

Fee, Gordon. *Gospel and Spirit: Issues in New Testament Hermeneutics.* Peabody, MA: Hendrickson, 1991.

Hyatt, Eddie L. *2000 Years of Charismatic Christianity.* Lake Mary, FL: Charisma House, 2002.

___. Hyatt, Eddie. *Discovering the Real Jesus.* Grapevine, TX: Hyatt Press, 2023.

___. Hyatt, Eddie. *Pursuing Power.* Grapevine, TX: Hyatt Press, 3014.

Hyatt, Susan. *In the Spirit We're Equal.* Dallas: Hyatt Publ., 1998.

Kung, Hans. *The Church.* Garden City, NY: Image Books, 1967.

___. *Christianity: Essence, History, and Future.* New York: Continuum, 1996.

___. Ed. *Apostolic Succession: Rethinking A Barrier to Unity,* New York: Paulist Press, 1968.

Lewis, C.S. *Mere Christianity.* Glasgow, England: Fount Paperbacks, 1977.

Luther, Martin. *Three Treatises.* Philadelphia: Fortress Press, 1970.

Neander, Augustus. *General History of the Christian Religion and Church.* 4 Vols. Trans. Joseph Torrey. Boston: Crocker & Brewster, 1853.

Nouwen, Henri, *In the Name of Jesus*. New York: Crossroad, 1989.

Schaff, Philip. *History of the Christian Church*. 8 vols. Grand Rapids, MI: Eerdmans, 1910.

Scholer, David. "Patterns of Authority in the Early Church." Vol. 1. *Authority and Governance in the Evangelical Covenant Church*. Chicago: Covenant Publ., 1993.

Stevenson, J. Ed. *Creeds, Councils, and Controversies* London: S.P.C.K. Holy Trinity Church, 1972.

Streeter, Burnett H. *The Primitive Church*. New York: MacMillan, 1929.

Suenens, Cardinal Leon Joseph. *Ecumenism and Charismatic Renewal: Theological and Pastoral Orientations*. London: Darton, Longman & Todd, 1978.

___. *A New Pentecost*. New York: Seabury Press. 1975.

Tierney, Brian, *Origins of Papal Infallibility*. Leiden, the Netherlands: E.J. Brill, 1972.

Von Campenhausen, Hans. *Ecclesiastical Authority and Spiritual Power in the Churches of the First Three Centuries*. (Stanford, CA: Stanford University, 1969.

About the Author

Dr. Eddie L. Hyatt is a veteran minister of the Gospel, having served as a pastor, teacher, and professor of theology in the U.S. and Canada and having ministered in India, Indonesia, England, Ireland, Sweden, Poland, and Bulgaria. His passion is to see authentic revival and reformation in the modern 21st century church.

Eddie holds a Doctor of Ministry from Regent University where he majored in church history and spiritual renewal. He also holds the Master of Divinity and a Master of Arts in Historical-Theology from Oral Roberts University. He has taught in the School of Theology at Oral Roberts University, Christ for the Nations Institute, and Zion Bible Institute. He has also been a guest lecturer at numerous educational institutions, including Oxford University in Oxford, England.

Eddie presently resides with his wife, Dr. Susan Hyatt, in Grapevine, TX where they carry on a ministry preaching, teaching, writing and publishing. His website is www.eddiehyatt.com and he can be contacted at dreddiehyatt@gmail.com.

Other Books by Eddie L. Hyatt

Pursuing Power is available only from the online bookstore at www.eddiehyatt.com. All other materials are available from the same site and from Amazon.

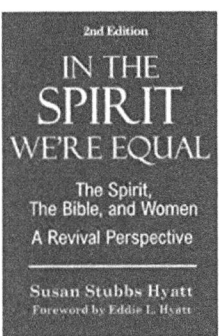

www.ingramcontent.com/pod-product-compliance
Lightning Source LLC
Chambersburg PA
CBHW031427040426
42444CB00006B/721